M000044251

mothers & daughters

Ariel Books

**Andrews McMeel
Publishing**

Kansas City

mothers & daughters

margaret lannamann

photographs by kerry giles

Photographs copyright © 2001 by Kerry Giles

Many thanks to Louise Egan for her invaluable help.

ISBN: 0-7407-0516-4
Library of Congress Catalog Card Number:
00-106913

introduction

Your mother—or your daughter—
is one of the most important fig-
ures in your life. From nursery rhymes
and walks in the park to confidences
shared during late-night talks, the bond
between you is built on shared experience and love, along with something
unique that one of the participants in
this book calls "an intuitive connection." You may at different times feel
affection, admiration, irritation, or
gratitude toward this individual, since
your relationship changes from month

to month, day to day—even hour to hour. However, the connection between the two of you is close and enduring, and your influence on one another is undeniable.

The mothers and daughters whose photographs appear in this book come from a variety of backgrounds and cultures, and they run the gamut in age from newborn to ninety. Despite these differences, when they talk about their relationships, certain phrases are repeated over and over: "I love her so much," "She's the best," and "We're

such good friends." As you read
through this book, pay tribute to the
mother or daughter—or both—who
has made such a difference in your life.

jennifer & naomi

Jennifer did a lot of baby-sitting during high school and college, but nothing prepared her for the delights of having a baby of her own. "I just love it," she says. "Every day brings something new."

Going back to work when Naomi was small was "the toughest thing I've ever done," Jennifer admits. But she likes the idea of Naomi seeing that her mother works, and fortunately, child care arrangements have gone smoothly. "Besides, now I appreciate the time I have with her so much more."

raven & alexis

raven & alexis

When Alexis was growing up, Raven, a single parent, chose to work in the nightclub business so she would be home when her children got up in the morning and when they came home from school in the afternoon. "This made me very popular with my friends," jokes Alexis.

Now that Alexis is grown, the two have their "Tuesday night ritual" when they have dinner together and catch up on each other's news. They also share a weekend beach house in the summer.

It is easy to see why Alexis is quick to say that her mother is her best friend.

"My mother raised us to be very open-minded," says Alexis. "She taught us that everyone sees things differently and that you shouldn't judge. She's un-biased, and very, very wise."

"The key to everything is good communication," Raven notes. "You have to be ready to listen. You can't just tell your children what to do. You must hear who they are and where they're coming from."

betsy & susannah

Susannah loves college life, but she misses her family when she's away. "This summer, my mother and I really bonded," she says. "We do so much together now—share books, go to coffee shops, exercise—even going to the grocery store together is fun."

Betsy echoes Susannah's sentiments. "We're very close. And I'm so pleased at what she's doing, at what she's becoming. I love the way she takes advantage of everything and gets so much out of every experience."

teresa & alice

teresa & alice

Teresa believes that it's extremely important for a woman to be independent. After she came to this country as a war bride from Panama, she took pride in working long and hard. "To do things right, you can never sit down," she says. Alice adds, "My mother taught me that you should be strong, you should have money of your own, and you should always remember who you are. And she doesn't just talk the talk, she walks it."

Teresa is the kind of person others go

to when they are in trouble, or when they have something joyful to share. Alice brings her positive outlook and generous, energetic spirit to this compatible pairing.

Alice's admiration of her mother is easy to see ("My mother is so cool—she's so up with the times, and she looks so good"), as is Teresa's pride in her daughter. Called Nana by most of this large family, Teresa is famous for flowers. "I love keeping my garden," she says. "I love to be outside with my family."

alice & talia

alice & talia

Like Teresa, Alice constantly passes bits of wisdom on to her daughter. As she has gotten older, Alice says she sees more clearly what's important and what's not. One of her maxims is that *everyone* is always welcome at her table. "It doesn't matter if the chairs match," she says with a smile.

Talia relishes the closeness and richness that her family provides. "There are so many sides to this family," she notes. What about arguments? "We'll have a big fight," she admits. "We don't hold back. But then we'll laugh about it five minutes later. Everyone really gets along very well."

Talia thinks she and her mother are alike in a lot of ways. "We pretend we're not, but we are," she jokes. Then she adds more seriously, "We're very blended."

Alice is full of admiration for her only daughter. "God has truly blessed her. She has so many talents. Now it's her turn to give something back to the planet."

nancy, amy julia, kate, brooks, & elly

nancy, amy julia, kate, brooks, & elly

"It seems we're always laughing," says Amy Julia. From the practical jokes this family loves to play on one another to the silly songs they make up to sing at special occasions, laughter runs continually through their day-to-day lives.

Nancy, the mom, tries to arrange family dinners as often as possible. "It gets harder as the girls get older," she admits, "but we do it whenever we can." Elly comments that when Amy Julia was married recently, "We all had such a good time. Shopping for all those clothes was so much fun."

Some of their warmest memories come from family vacations. Kate remembers "a week in the Caribbean when we'd all go swimming at sunset each evening. It was magical." Other favorite times are weekends spent at their summer house, "tickle nights" as they were growing up, and watching home movies together.

"We have a great time together," says Brooks. "And somehow, we bring out the best in each other."

nidza & ashley

"Ashley taught me to laugh again," Nidza says of her daughter. "She's funny, and she makes people happy."

Ashley and Nidza enjoy shopping ("Ashley is even better at it than me," says Nidza) and in-line skating in the park. "Mom too!" adds Ashley.

Although Nidza leaves no doubt about who's in charge, she clearly treats Ashley with respect. When conflicts come up, the two usually work them out. "We're both stubborn," admits Nidza, "but someone will give in."

brigid, lila, mumu, & collette

brigid, lila, mumu, & collette

"We are truly an international family," says Brigid. Her three daughters, as well as one son, were adopted at birth from other countries. "Lila and Mumu are Korean, and Collette is from Paraguay. We pay a lot of attention to their cultural heritage, incorporating customs and holidays and so forth into our family traditions." The girls attend schools that have an international flavor, and have friends from all over the world.

On the occasion of Collette's adoption (she is the youngest), the whole family spent a month in Paraguay. That time was, says Brigid, "one of the greatest bonding times for our family." She will never forget how gentle and kind the women there were, and how close her family became.

Some favorite family times are dinners together, evenings spent watching old movies, and visiting museums. "One thing I love is reading to Collette," says Lila. "And we love to joke around," adds Mumu. "We do that a lot."

erica, ann marie, & julia

We *love* to talk," says Erica. "And we talk a lot." But this family does a lot of other things together, like music, painting, yoga, reading, and sewing. "Julia is amazing," says older sister, Ann Marie, admiringly. "She is so good at art and music and dancing."

Erica says that being a mother has been an experience of "perpetual growth" for her. "The girls have truly reinspired me in things I used to love. Their enthusiasm has given me renewed vigor."

madeleine & christina

madeleine & christina

Although Madeleine and Christina look surprisingly alike, Madeleine thinks they are very different in character. "Christina is much more independent than I was at her age," says Madeleine. "She doesn't hesitate to run off and do something on her own. I would never have done that. But I think her strength of character will make her life easier as she gets older."

Madeleine says that Christina, even at this early age, is very athletic. "She's quite advanced physically, and is into everything. She loves to take things apart. And for some reason, she loves jewelry—beads and things like that."

Madeleine has elected to stay at home while Christina is young. Because she has an older son, she knows how fleeting the early years are. "It's important to be here," she says. "Everything changes so fast."

Keeping up with a two-year-old is no easy task, she admits. "Christina is always on the go. These days, I put a new value on finding free time!"

cecile, anne sophie, alice, caroline, & emmanuelle

Every summer, Cecile and her four daughters go back to their native France where they spend a month at the seaside, catching up with family members. "We go fishing and crabbing," Cecile says. "And we see our cousins," adds Anne Sophie.

With four young daughters, Cecile admits that life is extremely busy. "But the older ones help with the younger ones," she says. "They are very affectionate and sweet together. They're not alike at all, but they get along well."

ann & rachel

ann *&* rachel

Because it's just the two of them (Ann chose to be a single mother from Rachel's birth), Ann and Rachel are very close. They have what Ann calls "an intuitive connection" that creates a special kinship between them.

"Sometimes it's hard," says Ann, "because if we have a conflict, there's no one else to go to. But we always work things out." Rachel agrees, adding firmly, "We don't believe in blame."

A favorite memory of Rachel's is the night she and her mother rented three old videos, brought home lots of take-out food, and stayed up half the night laughing and crying over the movies—and eating every bit of the goodies. The two also enjoy hanging out in bookstores and museums, going to amusement parks, playing board games—and climbing trees!

Now that Rachel is growing up, Ann says, "She needs me just as much as before but in a different way. I want to be around as much as I can because this is the age for passing things on."

colleen, heather, & brooke

colleen, heather, & brooke

"I've always been astounded at what my mother can do," says Brooke. "She organizes our family in an amazing way, and she's always there for us. She's like a super superwoman."

Heather adds, "I have these childhood memories of her asking us to get our things together and climb into the car. She'd take us to Florida or some other totally unexpected place. It was great. I can't say enough positive things about my mom."

Of course, there have been tough

times. "But the good overshadowed everything," says Heather. "Now we spend most of our time together laughing," says Brooke.

Colleen thinks that being a mother to Heather and Brooke helped her to have insight into herself. "The girls were very introspective as they were growing up. They had a major role in helping me figure out who I was," she explains. And now that they're off on their own? "That's our job, isn't it? Love 'em, and then launch 'em."

diana & sylvia

Diana, who is a textile designer, is delighted by the creative talent she sees in her daughter, Sylvia. "She's really good at arts and crafts. Because of my job, there is always a lot of fabric around, and Sylvia makes the most amazing things."

Now that Sylvia is growing up and becoming more independent, Diana finds her to be sensible and reasonable. "She's wise beyond her years," she says proudly. "I feel so fortunate in having a daughter."

paula & tara

paula & tara

Paula and Tara may not see each other for several weeks at a time, but they talk on the phone at least once or twice a day. "In fact," Paula laughs, "I call Tara every morning to wake her up!" What do they do when they're together? They might share a meal, go shopping, or just cuddle on the couch together watching a movie. "We're pretty much in tune with each other," says Paula.

Tara is quick to say that she has the best mother anyone could ask for. "As you grow up, you see yourself through your parents' eyes," she explains. "My mother taught me to love myself because she loved me so much. I never had to be what she wanted me to be. She always let me be my own person."

When Tara was younger, she and Paula were able to talk through most of the problems that came up. And now that Tara is grown, their relationship is stronger than ever. "Without a doubt," says Tara, "my mother is my best friend."

ronita, madhuri, & monjori

Ronita and her two daughters are completing a two-year stay in the United States before returning to India. During their stay, they have explored much of the country. "Disneyland was *fun!*" Madhuri says.

Ronita has been happily married since 1986. "It was arranged. We never spoke to each other, never dated—I feel like laughing, it worked so well." Even so, she says she would like her daughters to decide for themselves whom they will someday marry.

antoinette, andrea,
nanette, lisa, & emily

antoinette, andrea, nanette, lisa, & emily

Antoinette, Nanette, and Emily live in the Northeast, and Andrea and Lisa live in California, so getting all three generations together is always a special occasion. "Our best times are probably when we're all sitting around the dining room table," says Andrea. "We all talk at the same time, but nobody minds." Sometimes they might take a walk or watch a parade—"It doesn't matter *what* we do," says Nanette. "It's doing it together that's important."

Lisa and Emily particularly enjoy spending time with Antoinette, their grandmother. Summers bring a week or two with everyone together, and include plenty of visits to the beach.

Antoinette cherishes the times she spends with her daughters. Not long ago, she and Nanette took a trip to Italy. They laughed and joked and had a wonderful time. "There's a certain point," she says, "when mothers and daughters stop being that and simply become good friends."

nanette & emily

I love being a mother," says Nanette, who has two sons in addition to her daughter, Emily. "I love seeing the world through my children's eyes, to see their curiosity and excitement." How has being a mother changed her? "I've learned patience, and to keep my work schedule flexible," she says.

Emily notes, "If I have trouble with my friends or at school, it always helps to talk with my mom. It's great because she's been through a lot of these same experiences."

andrea & lisa

andrea & lisa

Although Lisa and her mother live in California, Lisa is attending college in the east where the rest of the family lives, so there has been lots of family visiting. "And Mom comes when she can," says Lisa.

Andrea marvels at the differences that having children has brought into her life. "All of a sudden, you think of the children first," she says. "Very easily, they become much more important than other things. And they stay that way."

"My mom and I are pretty different," says Lisa. After thinking for a moment, she adds, "But we both like to help people out when they need something. And we're both kind of quiet. When we're out somewhere, we like to sit and watch people."

"There's an old-fashioned soda fountain we like to go to," says Andrea. "It's almost become a tradition. When Lisa's home, we'll go there." "And we like to putz around doing regular, everyday things," says Lisa.

madge & linda

I admire Mother," says Linda. "She's very strong and resilient. She's also fearless—many years ago she took her family to Argentina to live. I was five at the time, and back then, traveling all that way was a pretty unusual thing."

Madge and Linda get together several times a month. They lunch and go to museums or the opera, or else they might just visit together at Madge's apartment, which is, according to Madge, "just like a gallery of family pictures."

esther & shaan

esther & shaan

"Shaan and I have a great capacity to work together," says Esther. "Whether it's cooking or some other chore, we help each other till it's done. We just click that way." Shaan adds, "Now that I have a baby of my own, it's so great when my mother's around. This generational thing is wonderful."

Before Shaan's son was born, Shaan and Esther would often go out to shows and literary readings. Now they tend to stay closer to home. "We play a lot of backgammon at the kitchen table," says Shaan. "We can talk and laugh for hours, playing off each other's energy."

"It's a joy when I visit my children now—and I visit them a lot," says Esther. "It's been wonderful to see them growing in grace and developing their own lives and values. Of course, raising them wasn't always easy! But if you're honest, if you're truthful—and I'm prayerful—and if you spend a lot of time with them, you can end up with this wonderful feeling of harmony."

tracy & lydia

"Even at eight months, Lydia is happy and full of life," says Tracy. "When she smiles, you see it from head to toe. She smiles with her whole body. And she's always laughed right out loud."

Lydia is also a snuggler. She loves being close to her mother, looking at picture books, and giving hugs. "She's such a fun, gregarious little girl," says Tracy. "I'll be going back to teaching next year, so being able to spend this time at home with her now is truly wonderful."

karen & jamielyn

karen & jamielyn

Karen, who was forty-three when Jamielyn was born, finds being a mother has caused her to grow tremendously. "I've done so much in my life, been in the Peace Corps, traveled, gotten my Ph.D. and such," she says, "but through Jamielyn I've learned so much more."

Jamielyn and Karen are very close. Are the two alike? "Definitely," says Jamielyn. In fact, Jamielyn believes she and her mother are soul mates. "Sometimes," she says, "we'll be sitting doing different things and we'll stop, look at each other, and say the exact same thing."

Among the activities they enjoy doing together are eating at exotic restaurants, biking, reading, and taking walks. They both love music, and because their tastes are a little different, each enriches the other when they share favorite pieces. "We grow and learn together," says Karen. "Jamielyn is like a bridge to the future for me. And I am like a bridge to the past."

This book is set in
Bembo and Poetica.

❧

Designed and typeset by Junie Lee Tait
in New York City